CPS-PEIRCE ES

32489109035243   577.34 DAV
How high in the rainforest? :

W9-AGF-812

DISCARD

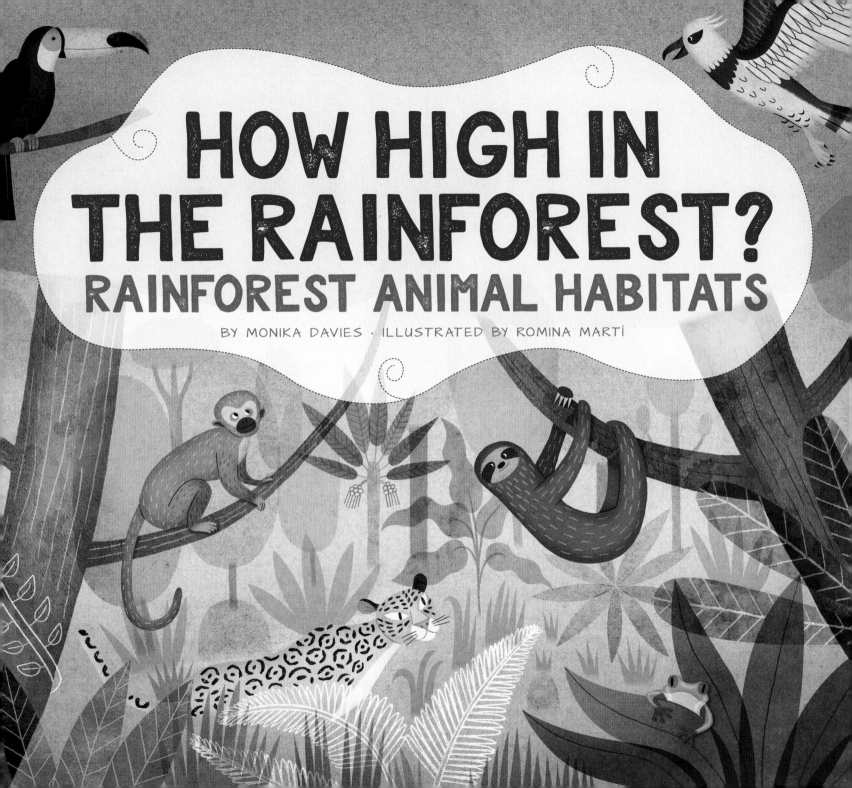

HOW HIGH IN THE RAINFOREST?
RAINFOREST ANIMAL HABITATS

BY MONIKA DAVIES · ILLUSTRATED BY ROMINA MARTÍ

Amicus Illustrated and Amicus Ink
are published by Amicus
P.O. Box 1329
Mankato, MN 56002
www.amicuspublishing.us

Copyright © 2019 Amicus. International copyright reserved in all
countries. No part of this book may be reproduced in any form
without written permission from the publisher.

Library of Congress Cataloging-in-Publication Data
Names: Davies, Monika, author. | Marti, Romina, illustrator.
Title: How high in the rainforest? : rainforest animal habitats /
    by Monika Davies ; illustrated by Romina Marti.
Other titles: Rainforest animal habitats
Description: Mankato, MN : Amicus Illustrated, [2019] | Series:
    Animals measure up | Audience: K to grade 3. | Includes
    bibliographical references.
Identifiers: LCCN 2017057979 (print) | LCCN 2017060823
    (ebook) | ISBN 9781681514697 (pdf) | ISBN 9781681513874
    (library binding) | ISBN 9781681523071 (pbk.)
Subjects: LCSH: Rain forest ecology—Juvenile literature. | Rain forest
    animals—Juvenile literature. | Animal behavior—Juvenile literature.
Classification: LCC QH541.5.R27 (ebook) | LCC QH541.5.R27 D38
    2019 (print) | DDC 577.34—dc23
LC record available at https://lccn.loc.gov/2017057979

Editor: Rebecca Glaser
Designer: Kathleen Petelinsek

Printed in the United States of America at
Corporate Graphics in North Mankato, Minnesota.

HC 10 9 8 7 6 5 4 3 2 1
PB 10 9 8 7 6 5 4 3 2 1

About the Author

Monika Davies has travelled to 38 countries around the
world, but still has not stepped foot in a rainforest. (It's on
the to-do list.) One day, she would like to meet a toucan in
person. Monika graduated from the University of British
Columbia with a bachelor of fine arts in creative writing.
She has written over eighteen books for young readers.

About the Illustrator

Romina Martí is an illustrator who lives and works in
Barcelona, Spain, where her ideas come to life for all
audiences. She loves to discover and draw all kinds of
creatures from around the planet, who then become the
main characters for the majority of her work. To learn
more, go to: rominamarti.com

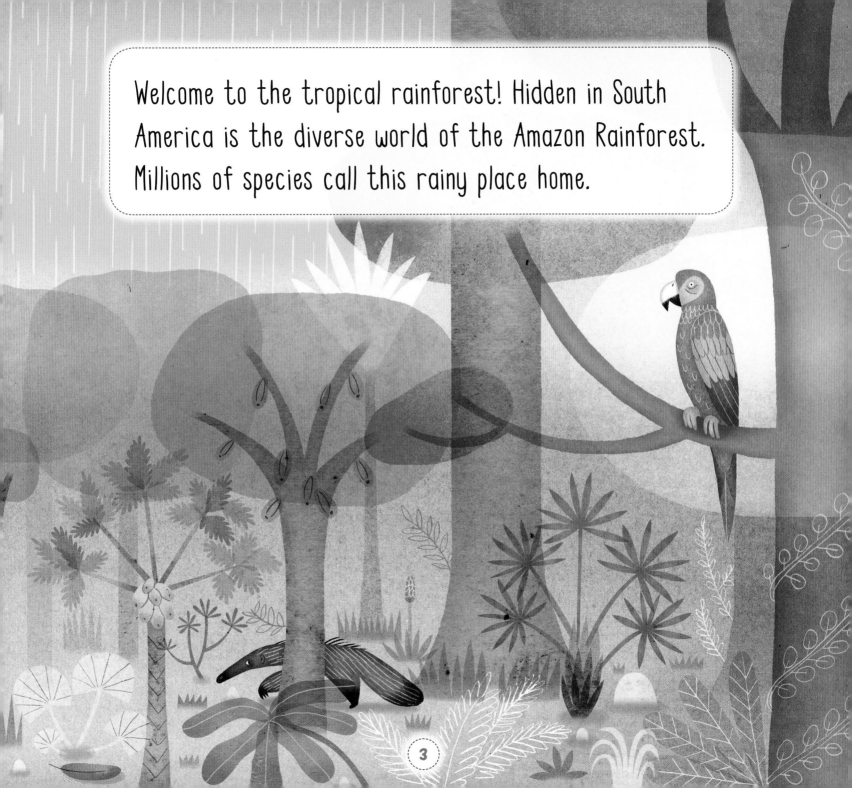

Welcome to the tropical rainforest! Hidden in South America is the diverse world of the Amazon Rainforest. Millions of species call this rainy place home.

Step inside! The forest floor is the bottom layer of the rainforest. Here, the sun barely shines through. Because it's so dark, not much grows here.

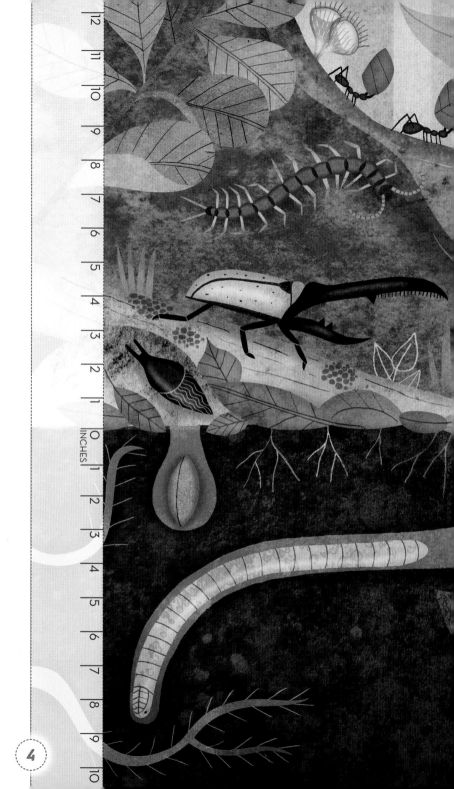

Hidden in the dirt are "recyclers." Centipedes, slugs, beetles, and termites eat dead leaves. Their poop adds nutrients to the soil.

The forest floor feeds many animals. Meet the giant armadillo. It's claws are built to dig. Armadillos enjoy tasty meals of beetles and other bugs. Wild pigs sniff out bugs and roots. Small rodents find food here, too.

The next layer is the understory. Here, shadows linger. Only a bit of sunlight peeks through. Plants must sprout wide leaves. This helps them soak up skinny rays of sun.

Red-eyed tree frogs may catch your eye. Their bright eyes surprise their enemies. They live here in the shadows. The humid air keeps the frogs' skin moist.

The shadows are also perfect for hunters. Jaguars crouch on tree branches. Then, *pounce!* They leap on their prey on the forest floor.

Higher up is the "roof" of the rainforest. Here, tree branches weave together. They form a thick covering called the canopy. The canopy is about as high as a 10-story building!

Sloths curl up in the treetops. Up here, they chew on a feast of leaves. When they sleep, their long claws hold them steady.

Animals and plants that live in the canopy are adapted for this high, wet layer. Leaves are shaped so rain drips off quickly. Animals that live this high can all fly, leap, or swing. Toucans soar past. Spider monkeys swing from tree to tree, looking for fruit.

Look up! Way up! At the tip-top of the rainforest is the emergent layer. Here, the trees can stretch up to 200 feet (60 meters) tall. It is hot, because these trees get full sun.

Up top, every day is different. Some days, the rains crash down. There are also many dry days. These tall trees have small, waxy leaves. This helps them retain water when it is dry.

To live this high, an animal must be nimble! Squirrel monkeys are light on their feet. They can run along thin branches.

230
FT
220
210
200
190
180
170
160
150

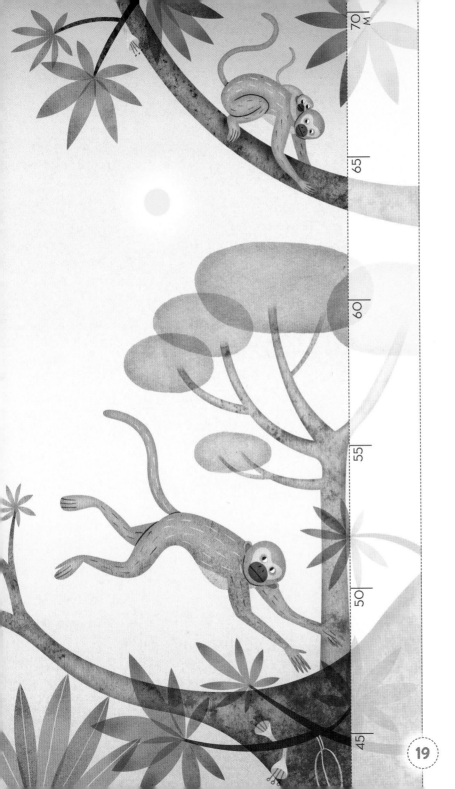

The harpy eagle perches up here. It can be hard for this bird to spot its prey. The tree tops are too thick. Instead, it uses its sharp hearing. It preys on sloths and other mammals.

You never know which animals you will meet in this wet world. Macaws soar up high. Iguanas hide in the trees. Capybaras roam the forest floor. So many species live in this tall, green oasis!

LAYERS OF A RAINFOREST

EMERGENT LAYER
100–200 FT
(30–60 M)

squirrel monkey

harpy eagle

CANOPY LAYER
16–100 FT
(5–30 M)

toucan

sloth

UNDERSTORY LAYER
0–16 FT (0–5 M)

jaguar

red-eyed tree frog

FOREST FLOOR
0 FT (0 M)

insects

giant armadillo

GLOSSARY

canopy The second-highest layer of the rainforest, where trees grow thick.

diverse Made up of things that are different from each other.

emergent layer The highest layer of the rainforest, made of the tallest trees.

forest floor The ground layer of the rainforest.

humid Having a lot of moisture in the air.

nutrient A substance that plants, animals, and people need to live and grow.

oasis A pleasant place that is surrounded by something unpleasant.

retain To continue to hold something (such as heat or moisture) as time passes.

understory The second-lowest layer of the rainforest, made of short shrubs.

READ MORE

Kopp, Megan. **What Do You Find in a Rainforest Tree?** New York: Crabtree Publishing, 2016.

Patkau, Karen. **Who Needs a Jungle?: A Rainforest Ecosystem**. Toronto: Tundra Books, 2012.

Tarbox, A.D. **A Rainforest Food Chain**. Mankato, Minn.: Creative Education, 2016.

WEBSITES

Amazon Rainforest – DK Find Out!

https://www.dkfindout.com/uk/animals-and-nature/habitats-and-ecosystems/amazon-rainforest/

Investigate the Amazon rainforest with this cool interactive map.

Journey into Amazonia – PBS

http://www.pbs.org/journeyintoamazonia/index.html

Put on your explorer cap and dive into the Amazon rainforest with this interactive experience.

Tropical Rain Forest – San Diego Zoo

http://animals.sandiegozoo.org/habitats/tropical-rain-forest

The animals of the rainforest world are a colorful bunch of characters!

Learn all about them at the San Diego Zoo's website.

Every effort has been made to ensure that these websites are appropriate for children. However, because of the nature of the Internet, it is impossible to guarantee that these sites will remain active indefinitely or that their contents will not be altered.